Diary of a MAD Black Woman!

A Memoir

by **Victoria Nkong**

Copyright © 2018 by Victoria Nkong

All rights reserved. Published by **The BRAG Media Company** & Printed in the United States of America. No part of this book may be reproduced, stored in a retrieval system, or transmitted in any form or by any means, electronic, mechanical, photocopying, recording, scanning, or otherwise, without the prior written permission, except in the case of brief quotation embodied in reviews or critical articles.

Disclaimer

The views expressed in this book are those of the author and are provided for motivational & informational purposes only. While every attempt has been made to provide information that is both accurate and effective, the author do not assume any responsibility for the use/misuse of the information.

This book may be ordered from booksellers or contact

info@qtabyevents.com

www.VictoriaNkong.com

Book and Cover design by

The BRAG Media Company

ISBN : 978-1719869454

Dedication

This book is dedicated to God who has always shown up for me at my lowest moments.

My beloved 23 children, my mother who went above and beyond to ensure that I use my energy positively; my family for being all that I have, my friend Alex who thought that my story was worth sharing and ensured we achieved this together.

My man, when he eventually finds me because he will be dealing with a handful.

To my partner at the Orphanage: Mr. Jegede Abiodun Paul the chairman of Japaul Group who has been such a motivation and every human being out there who is seeking to find themselves and seemingly misunderstood for being a bundle of talent and energy.

Preface

Life is a journey, for some people it is fast and for others it seems slow.

I have learnt to own my journey, I have learnt to walk and work at my pace, ensuring however that my pace is my best.

Through the last 30 years of my life, I have answered one recurrent question at different stages:

"HOW DO YOU DO IT?"

Initially, I always wondered what they were talking about, how could people be fascinated by my everyday reality? But I have now grown to accept the fact that there must be a mystery somewhere somehow, there must be something that I am getting right in the midst of all my wrongs, there is definitely something that someone out there could learn from my journey.

It has been 30 years only but it has been extremely eventful. I have produced great events, TV shows e.t.c telling other peoples stories….but never mine.

Diary of A Mad Black Woman is an extract from a global anthology that I co-authored alongside 20 brave women from different parts of the world.

It is my memoire, it is filled with my flaws, but most importantly it contains the secret to how I OVERCAME and continue to OVERCOME.

The Introduction...

My name is Victoria Nkong, Daughter, Sister, Mother, Charity Administrator, Events Producer, TV Producer, Public Relations Expert, Talent Manager, Public Speaker, and Natural Counselor.

I also write for the love of writing and oh...I'm probably a wife-to-be someday...it took me a while to come to terms with the fact that being a wife could be a pleasant part of a woman's' life due to an experience that left myself and my entire family chattered, an experience which seemed to be the seal that I needed to realize that pain could be the fastest catalyst for growth and self-development once embraced and appropriately dealt with.

I felt I had successfully escaped marriage and didn't need it since I am a mother to several children at the orphanage already but I have come to realize how much we all need a companion to share our lowest and highest moments with, when all the work and success is achieved, we need to go home to that someone or at least have a voice at the other end of the phone jubilating with you right? Whatever be the case...I'm a bit indifferent and please don't judge me.

I refer to myself as "The Best Thing that Happened

to the World" not in arrogance but because it is a way of reminding myself daily that despite my limitations I am the best version of me and this enables me go the extra-mile to actually be the best thing that happened to everyone that meets me.

As C.E.O of Qtaby Events and Entertainment, I double up HR functions...yes...I have to manage a wide range of human egos and mood swings and still get them to be the best version of themselves.

As a Talent Manager, it is even worse; branding people into the limelight and managing the ego that comes with their new status as well as managing their fans in some cases; ensuring I project a positive image of them all the time, keeping the smile on my lips even at moments when I would love to just scream and throw tantrums.

Switching between the sweet manager and confidant for my Talents as well as being the firm, mean manager when it is time to correct their misdeeds and put things into proper perspective. Realizing after a while that the timid girl or boy who you sacrificed 4years of your life nurturing has finally gained acceptance and is becoming a brand; this is supposedly good news except that that timid girl now acts like she has ants in her brain because she suddenly has an audience.

I have learnt through life to be the sweetest to the sweet and gal to the bitter, maintaining the balance is unarguably one of the most challenging parts of my job but I have also since realized that I was born to do this, it is my calling, it is the life I chose and somewhat the life that I am stuck with.

I operate in the background most times even when something keeps tucking at me from the inside suggesting that the limelight is where I belong, at what age am I going to give into that little inner voice? Soon? Later? Never? Oh well... I am that little girl on the inside that comes out exuding so much confidence and behaving like I have got everything in control and I can look the world in the eye, while in truth I am very shy on the inside and wishing that someone else would take away the responsibility of the front line from me.

My life is so full of drama that I sometimes wonder how anyone could live like I do; constantly running between changing diapers and playing loving mother to 23 children on the average, and trying to keep up with the glamour involved in strutting the red-carpet while trying to be the modest Christian woman...no stop button at all...the phone calls on the steering, the switch in accent and tone, running from the children's play room to the office to ensure that the phone isn't pulled off my ear by one of my beautiful children in the course of an important business conversation, there are bills to pay so we need this money and I need to convince the world that I am serious minded…By the way have you seen me dance? Michael Jackson and Shakira have got nothing on me, even though my dancing career is mostly restricted to my bedroom and my car because in truth I can't survive one complete hour in a club, the noise is just not meant for me.

Coming from a family of educationists, education was a very important part of my childhood. We were all sent off to school at a very early age, constantly monitored to ensure that our academics flourished, I was constantly underage through all my stages in school, younger than 99% of my schoolmates at every point, went ahead to obtain my 1st degree quite early and decided that I wanted to be independent immediately. I had chosen a field of study that didn't inspire a lot of confidence in my family and they wanted me to go back to school immediately for another degree while I wanted to prove to them that I would excel with my chosen field, with or without a second degree. Besides I liked money too much and had been dreaming of beginning to make my own money so I was not going to let other people live their dreams through me. Off I went, right into the world to make that money and make a difference in my world.

Before you begin to play with this idea of rebellious financial independence in your head, wait and read this carefully "*the road to financial independence is rough and tough, it was not and still isn't a walk in the park for me, the hurdles and bumps are countless,* especially for someone with my temperament, you will have long days and lonely nights, you will wake up some day and call yourself a failure; hate yourself and everyone around you, this is not a threat, it is the reality of most budding entrepreneurs... but eventually it will be worth it all if you keep at it with determination..

Finally, I am currently at that place where I think I have control over my emotions, I am sure that we need each other to survive but I am also aware that I will be just fine without you. My heart is still very tender; however, I have been able to build the much needed protective wall around it to keep me sane.

I have transitioned through several phases in life, from the little mummy and daddy's girl to the vocal teenager, through to the independent woman initially facing the world eyeball to eyeball, then realizing I should have probably faced the world chest up before looking it straight in the eye. I have had my experiences, exciting, rough, tough and liberating; in all of these, I believe that is what makes me Victoria Nkong and I would never choose another life.

If you are stuck with four personalities in one and trying to decipher how to make sense out of it, hold my hand and let us walk that road together, I have been there and it is my current reality, always remember "Impossible Is Nothing."

Table of Contents

Chapter 1: Somewhere In Africa, A Mad Woman is Born...1

Chapter 2: My Principles...................................11

Chapter 3: My Entrepreneurial Journey............36

Chapter 4: Purpose, Gifts & Miracles................63

Chapter 5: My Realities....................................74

Chapter 6: Happiness, Self Love & Summary..86

My Favourite Quotes 94

About The Author...96

Chapter 1:

Somewhere In Africa, A Mad Woman is Born...

My mother had five girls already and desperately wanted a male child, when she had me, a mischievous elder sister tried to convince them that I was a boy and I was nick-named "Chikito", a name which I grew up fighting against.

Mine was a very exciting childhood with several phases. I am the last child of a very large polygamous and multi-ethnic family. So I mostly had three homes, the home from my mother's point of view, the home from my father's point of view and the home from their joint point of view. One thing they had in common is that they were firm believers and worshippers of God and went the extra mile to instill the same values in us.

While mum was a lot on the reserved side, having had a partly western upbringing and preferred to keep her circle closed; dad came from a largely polygamous African family and operated an open door policy. Dad and mum were both educationist and dad at the time was the State Director for Education so we were all sent off to school at a very tender age, not to mention the fact that our house was a hub for everyone that came from the village and needed to get some education in the city.

This was my first multi-personality experience and the point where I learnt everything about love affairs and relationships and realized how I will want to be treated because unknown to dad, the rooms in the boys quarters which he gave to these guests, had become a playfield for all sorts of relationships. Mum was very sensitive to this fact and I remember her vividly giving us moral talks about relationships, I remember being taught that sex was for marriage and not before, that a woman is to carry herself in a certain way that attracts dignity...oh yes, this stuck as well and who will believe that in 2018 there's a grown woman somewhere who still holds onto such theories?

I remember being made to study "everything a teenage girl should know and everything a teenage boy should know" over and over again hence my capacity to hold back and refuse to be treated like some of those girls that came to sleep over illegitimately in our boys quarters. Oh my sweet mother, I remember mum waking me up by 1am when I was just 12 years old and asking my elder sister and I to follow her to her room for a conversation. My sister and I were really worried, we got into mums room and she brought out a condom, gave us a looonnnnggg talk, asked questions about abstinence and started painstakingly putting us through the process of using condoms then going ahead to tell us how wrong it will be to need to use it before marriage. I was furious, what could I have done to deserve this from my mum? Why wake me up from sleep to give me this uncomfortable and gory talk???

Years later, I cannot be too sure if there isn't a negative side to this as I am constantly on the defensive towards any man that tries to come close and being in a relationship is such an effort for me right now even though I know that there is so much love in my heart waiting to be expressed but I know for a fact that this helped me protect myself from most of the misadventures that I could have had as a young inexperienced girl.

On the other hand, I quickly imbibed a culture of accommodating whoever is in need and sharing as much as possible since my family house was like a shelter for the homeless. Again I grew up being quite flexible with accommodating people to an extent that this kind attribute of mine will later get me into trouble a number of times.

Respect for elders was also a strong point in my home, If I ever got into a squabble with anyone senior to me, be it my sisters, the house keeper or one of our august visitors, I was made to apologize and taught that it was the right thing to do. I was trained to show love and care, respect my elders but I was also taught to fight for my right when necessary by my "Margaret Thatcher elder sister who spent a lot of time explaining to us why we shouldn't allow ourselves to be taken for granted. I will greet everyone and try as much as possible to be modest and I cannot understand why the children that walk around today will look at an elder straight in the eyes and walk past them….I feel quite uncomfortable about this and feel that as a people we have failed, we have become so materialistic that we have taught even our growing children that affection and respect is directly dependent on societal status, financial capability and show of affluence irrespective of how the money was made.

I grew up to several vacations, Christmas and birthdays being special, loyalty to family and friends being important e.t.c; all these have remained a huge part of me as I even go the extra mile in expressing my loyalty: my friends enemy is my enemy, simple! It feels extremely disappointing when I do not get that in return from my friends though.

There were highs and lows. On one occasion, mum had been transferred away from dad by her office when we were very young and we had to stay with mum, there was this drift between both of them and mum had to suddenly take up all our bills singlehandedly and this affected mum financially. I spent those years watching my mum sacrifice everything that she had to ensure that we were comfortable and we didn't lack any of the good things that we had been accustomed to in life...I couldn't get a clear picture then because I was very young but we all noticed it was tough and she was making a great effort to keep away the struggle from us. I remember my mum selling off all her jewelry at a point and going without jewelry for a period, I remember asking her once why she no longer wore earrings and she held me closely and said "I decided to take a break for a while my darling" I remember the tears in her eyes as she answered. I remember her having to take over our school fees for a while and how she insisted that we will not be moved to cheaper schools and how she was determined to pay the bills against all odds. Determined to not lower the quality of life that we were used to either, she put in her all to ensure that the birthday parties for each of us were never skipped, a new dress for every festivity and those nice family holidays were maintained even though we all couldn't go at the same time anymore as we now had to go in batches.

Years later I came to understand and interpreted that phase of my life through the country song "my coat of many colors" with the lines that sang: I thought of all the love that was sewn with every stitch" "one is poor, only if you chose to be" "although we had no money but riches I could see in my coat of many colors that my mama made for me" *I learnt in those years that your greatest wealth isn't money but the people in your life that truly love and care about you.*

I learnt to look beyond wealth and physical possessions but to value people by the innate substance that made them who they are. Even when things blossomed again and we were one happy family, the marks from these lessons had been imprinted on the forever borders of my soul already.

The fun moments, the laughter, the quarrels, we had a name for dad and we will sit and speak about him, even in his presence and he will be unable to decipher that he is the subject of discussion. Then my first phase of growing up happened, I got into secondary school and asked to be put in boarding house, packed my bags and headed off to school only to realize that I had a lot of catching up to do, I was at a stage where I had elder ones bath me, take care of my clothes e.t.c at home and suddenly I now had to take care of senior students in school fetching water for them, doing their laundry and even organizing their wardrobe. The first three years of boarding school are the reason I will never forget my dad, very supportive but also very dedicated to putting things straight. I will come up with all sorts of excuses, forge the signature of the boarding mistress, and pretend to be seriously sick e.t.c all in a bid to go home. I looked so innocent and believable that no one would have imagined the level of mischief I employed just to get away from school. Fun memories indeed but then it helped me recognize one of my strengths; *"I would find a solution no matter how tough a situation is"*

I remember trying to leave school in JSS3, being unable to pass through the gate, a friend and I resolved to go through a forest that was located at the back of the school where a lot of locals from a nearby village had small farms close to some streams.

We walked our way towards the hills in our school wear and found somewhere in one of the farms where we quickly changed into our night gowns to enable us look like some of the villagers farming. A security man from school seemed to have seen us and got suspicious so he walked into the farms towards us, my heart was on a marathon even as we both maintained a very calm disposition, we started plucking leaves off a tree pretending to be unbothered about the approaching security man.

He got to us and asked what we were doing and my friend answered casually "our mother asked us to pluck some leaves for her" she spoke in the local dialect (which I couldn't speak by the way) and that was all the security man needed to convince him, he waved good bye and left us alone, by this time my heart was on the last lap of a million meters race, I died a hundred times and woke up. As soon as he left, I told my friend we had to hurry, we ran through the hills, realized the path was very undulated and very scary while the walk will later become almost unending. We helped some of the villagers carry their stuff in order to blend further, walked for about 3hours before getting back into civilization. Unfortunately for us, a heavy downpour started at that time, my regret on the entire adventure was intense, I managed to find my way home after the rains only to meet my father at home angrily asking why I was home from school again. I lied that I was sent away from school because my name was found on the list of people who had not paid their tuition fees, my dad was livid; why will the school send children home so late in the day? Why was his daughter sent home despite the fact that her fees had been paid long ago?

I was bundled back to school very early the next morning and my dad asked to see the school Administrator, she bluntly told him that there had been no fee drive and she knew nothing about what he was saying, then I was invited to recount my story "dear lord, I thought to myself, if you see me through this I promise to never tell lies again or escape from school...I will leave the rest of the story to your imagination.

Most of my values, ethos and principles stem from my childhood and this woman that I have become who is constantly seeking to ensure that there is a balance in life resonates the constant change between being daddy's girl and bro's side chick, taking after mum, ensuring that everyone is happy but also ensuring that everyone did what they are supposed to do, being firm and respecting principles and values...one thing I have prayed constantly for, is the ability to embed in my children the values that my mother embedded in us.... I think my childhood was priceless and I owe my children nothing less.

I hold my family so dear to my heart, I LOVE EACH OF THEM so much that at times it is almost a flaw; I also accord the same amount of respect to other people's families as that is the training that we got. No matter what you do, do not touch my family as it is my weak point and I may be unable to forgive you.

My family is my support system and I wonder what my life will be without them.

For every parent out there, remember that childhood is the formative part of a child's life, your child's behavior, values and personality is shaped within this time. In all you do, remember that you will never get a second chance at training your child and preparing your child for adulthood so make the best out of their childhood, create the right memories and imprint the right values in them, by so doing, you will avoid the stress of doing damage control when the child is older, you will save yourself the heartache of behavioral problems and troubled adolescence in your child; you will also save the society of the nuisance value that comes with a broken adolescent.

Your family is your primary responsibility as charity truly begins at home in this case.

Chapter 2:

My Principles...

Every human being must have some principles by which they live. Your inner core must have some principles imprinted in them to guide it, these principles could be formed through personal experiences or other peoples experiences. In all, *KNOW WHO YOU ARE.*

The Art of Living Naked

How else can nakedness be explained apart from being in your "Adam after the apple state?" Why will anyone want to live naked? On a more serious note, I see being "Naked" as being in your most transparent state, in that place where you're not ashamed of your vulnerability, inadequacies or shortcomings. Being Naked is getting to that point where you are unapologetically you, uncensored, where you have learnt to accept your reality. It is a state of bliss that every human-being needs to experience, as it is only in this state that you can live your best life and be open to experience new variables that can truly make you live and perhaps be better. I have learnt the art of being NAKED and it has been my winning tool and my greatest survival tool since I mastered the art.

I am not afraid to tell a person that I didn't make it this time, but I have learnt from my mistake and I will put in effort to make it next time. Yes I failed, but I intend to defy all odds to excel next time! Or I'm broke, but I have realized it is very inconveniencing, so I am working hard to never get broke again.

I see being naked as finally getting to a place of actual maturity in life. Love me the way I am? Welcome to my "queendom", think I should change a few things about my life and the way I operate? Okay, I will try but I don't intend to try out everybody's suggestion less I build a confused personality, I also do not hope to attain perfection as that will take my humanity away. I want to remain Victoria, sharpened through life's experiences, fortified from the fire of the good, the bad and the ugly.

The first step to being naked is staying true to who you are, being sincere with yourself, accepting the truth about your reality and being bold enough to confront it.

There is no such thing as a perfect life, do not let anyone deceive you by making you think that they have a perfect life while you don't, accept your truth, outline what needs to change and work towards it, your imperfections make you human, do not let anyone take away your humanity by making you feel the need to seem perfect.

Beyond everything else, being true to yourself comes with an unimagined peace; it is like self-rediscovery and opens you to the possibility of building yourself into a better person. There is so much that we lose from being covered, the effects are mostly negative than positive. You end up living someone else's life by trying to conform to a certain image that you think the person finds desirable.

You would have never really lived if you exit this world without getting to the point where you feel comfortable enough to be you and express yourself candidly through your actions, your works and your ambition for there-in lies the true essence of your existence, your talent and your real ability to impart the world.

Now that you and I have understood the concept of Nakedness, it will be easier for you to take this ride with me as I explicitly take you through my journey of how I became unstoppable, how I learnt to look beyond immediate situations and find the ray of light in every darkness, how I manage to rock this crazy roller-coaster life and personality and remain sane.

The notion of impossibility lies only in your head

my dear, for me, I have long realized that IMPOSSIBLE IS NOTHING.

Giving

God loves a cheerful giver; do not give with a grudge in mind. Somehow these simple words started guiding my existence from a very early age, I would give till I have no more. My siblings knew this part of me and they would take advantage of it to the letter. We all had individual pocket money but my pocket money belonged to everyone, they will ensure that mine is spent before they all start using theirs while I stayed empty. I would pretend that I was not hungry till everyone was done eating and either wanted a part of my meal or not.

My dad would say to me repeatedly: Victoria look after yourself and be healthy enough so that you can look after others. He dropped me off in school one morning and had to scream from the car "Victoria don't give your money to Joy today oh" Joy is my immediate elder sister who was in the same school as myself then. Everyone turned around to look and I could hear people laughing.

Twenty years later, I have not changed much from that girl that likes to give till I am burnt out. I still believe in giving and I know that we rise by lifting others. I will however like to maintain that it is important to look after yourself properly because a drowning soul cannot save another from drowning.

Giving is not only about finances but it also involves your time, your knowledge, your assets as well as your heart. However, avoid burnout, give yourself a chance to stay alive so that you can help give more people life.

Spiritual Beliefs

I am a Christian by birth, upbringing and conviction; however I am not a very religious person. I have come to see myself as a difficult Christian having had the opportunity to be exposed to a few other non-conventional Christian doctrines. I choose to let my inner man decipher what message is for me and what message is not for me. I am that ardent believer that will not simply take a standpoint because a certain Christian leader said so. I look at love as the greatest religion and I believe that the answers to our entire unanswered spiritual questions are living within us.

I try to respect people's differences in their spiritual beliefs and I try not to impose mine on anyone, I stay away from fanatics as I perceive them as the most dangerous and backward people in the world. I have had strong spiritual encounters that have formed the basis for my current beliefs and this has helped me build a direction in my spiritual life.

To everyone who cares to listen, I will like to

convince you that God actually exist and your relationship with him is best experienced in your personal closet. I have built my own unique relationship with him and it has been my winning factor through life's journey.

I will share a personal experience here and I know that this will arouse mixed reactions but remember that it is my memoire and I promised to be naked with you right?

I drove home one Friday from the orphanage in a very sober state of mind, almost depressed. I had just N5,000 left in my bank account and I had two children on admission in the hospital with several needs to attend to. The chairman of the orphanage, my partner was not in town and I did not want to disturb him with money issues. I got home and asked my security man to leave the generator off as I did not want noise and I felt like staying in the dark. I laid down on my bed thinking hard. I realized I could not ask anyone for a loan as it just wasn't my style. I was really troubled and I eventually got on my knees and started praying and questioning God. While still praying, my phone started ringing; it was one of my former business partners from another country with whom I had not spoken for about two years. I was so irritated, why was he calling me? I put my phone on silence and continued praying asking God for help. The phone kept ringing till I was done with prayers and so I decided to pick the call, he briefed me about a project for MTN and he wanted me to handle an aspect of the project, he asked that we put our grievances behind us and make things work. At the end of that phone call, 40,000USD was transferred to my account as deposit for a project which was to commence two months later, with a further 80,000USD later that week.

That was God showing up for me directly, it was his way of telling me that when he shows up for me, he shows up in grand style and all I need to do is to believe in him and do his will.

A lot of you may like to call it a coincidence but I know that whenever I get on my knees and genuinely cry to God, he shows up dramatically; immediately.

I have also distanced myself from my beliefs on different occasions and realized that seeking Gods face actually works better for me because when I ask questions I receive answers, I have had my encounters that confirm that God exists.

Whatever you do, know who you believe in and stick to him, it is dangerous to work around without considering the person that holds the essence of your existence.

However, I will like to add that "religion" is different from "Christianity" You could be religious without being a firm believer, know the difference and choose wisely where you belong.

Finances....

In the course of life, I have held on to the definition of wealth as a calculation of the number of lives that you have touched and influenced positively as opposed to the general concept of wealth being calculated by affluence. Affluence again is very relative because for a man whose dream had always been to drive a Mercedes, as soon as he acquires the Mercedes and enough money to maintain it over a period, he has attained his desired point of wealth whether or not the cost of his Mercedes can only replace the tyre of another man's Bentley.

Of course financial independence is a must for me, I love the good things of life for sure, and I know they were created for my comfort. I like to be able to pay for what I want, not just what I need, and yes I like to be able to pay for what I want at the very time I want it.

Every human being owes himself a moral responsibility to earn the money that he needs. Even from a moral point of view, you need the money to be able to touch lives and affect society positively.

I learnt from an early age to work for my earnings, I was literarily in a hurry to attain financial independence and I remember taking a job once while in college just so that I could earn my little something. I was determined at that time to not be anyone's responsibility as soon as I was done from college, so I went job hunting and eventually my dream job found me at the time and the pay was just what I had dreamt of as my first pay. I quickly tried to prove to my family that I had arrived and I will send gifts to everyone at the end of the month…everyone except my bank account. I went by the logic that "money was made to pay for needs and not to become a need on its own" This is true in a way, except that we also need to have some savings for the rainy day.

All was well until I decided to become an entrepreneur without ever considering what the true sense of the word meant. I registered a company with my little savings and decided to pilot a TV reality show using the contacts that I had made in the course of my entertainment sojourn and the thin knowledge that I had garnered at the time. It was a roller coaster of expenses and big dreams that always seemed to collapse right in my face. Of course my motive was noble, I had made good contacts and some know how, there were young people who didn't have the opportunities I had early in life but had the zeal and needed to work to earn a living; why couldn't I create job opportunities for these people and help them earn a living? Why couldn't I become that bridge between them and their dreams while achieving my own dreams? However I forgot that it will take more than just the passion and the know how to get me there. At the end of one year, I had finished my savings, I was totally broke and I hadn't gotten a sponsor or partner to invest in my project. The months that followed were horrendous but at least I learnt to suffer and keep a smile on after what will seem like my worst financial mistake.

However as stubborn and determined as I am, I will rather die than give up on my dreams, after all I know deep within that I am not a looser. So I held on to my dreams and devised a new means of survival each time until destiny took me to meet certain people in life that were instrumental to the game change in my life and business.

Several years later, I have learnt that financial planning is a very vital part of life.
- Money does not need to be your primary focus but you do need to have stable finances.
- There will be ups and downs, but maintain a certain threshold as much as you can.
- Do not lend out money that you cannot part with.
- Do not make an effort to show off your finances, make an effort to acquire and plan your finances.

Remember; human relationship is just as important as financial stability, some people think that human relationship is more important or less important but I maintain that it is just as important, if you are sick and helpless in your bed at home, you need a human being that cares enough about you to check on you and realize that all is not well, then the person can arrange for your medical care before your money can work for you by paying the bills; on the other hand, if you have plenty of money saved up and no one cares about you enough to check on you and help transfer you to a hospital for healthcare, your money will not lift you up from the bed and take you to the hospital, at the hospital, you also need money to pay the bills so please maintain a balance.

Beauty

I'm in love with my looks most of the time, except when I add some belly-fat that stops me from wearing those bodycon dresses and tops that I love so much, it almost feels depressing at times but I remind myself that God did a great job even though I feel like I could have done with a few more inches in terms of my height and there were years in the past when I dwelt a bit on that and had a few comments from friends but hey...the six inches and 12 inches heels have long solved that problem.

I am a 5.7, brown skinned, quite curvy behind with a pair of very beautiful eyes...I remember growing up and having my big sister taunt me very often about my eyes, whenever I upset her, she'll roll her palms into mini rolls and place them on her eyes and say "frog eyes, or big eyes like owl: e.t.c but interestingly those eyes eventually became one of the most striking features on my face and I get lots of compliments about my eyes daily. I think every human being decides how they want to look as we have the liberty to look a million dollar as well as the liberty to look like trash...I generally dress to suit my mood and as always I rock the best me anytime.

I love to look good and to be dressed in a particular way but nothing completes it as much as an expensive fragrance. It even changes my accent and thought process dramatically. I have made a cautious effort to accept myself as I am and I think I am very much at peace with my looks at the moment.

Generally I appreciate beauty from the content rather than the cover even for the opposite sex, I am not very much into looks but a lot more into innate substance, no that is a lie, I am actually into both, there needs to be a bit of good looks besides the intelligence and the good heart. However, you are more likely to get my attention with a smart conversation rather than a nice shirt.

My advice to everyone generally is to work towards getting the body that they desire, if you need to put in time at the gym, please do, if you need to diet, go ahead, do what you need to do to achieve your dream bod, you owe yourself that. I personally won't go under the knife to achieve body goals but that is because I can't stand the thought of being cut even for serious health issues how much less for getting a great body when I know I can achieve that otherwise. Something that helps though, is knowing how to dress to accentuate the best attributes of your body, once you master that art, you will have less to worry about getting the right body, every "body" is the right body but please do not go overweight for health reasons.

A little secret to keep in mind is the fact that your confidence and charisma is your first cloak, people will generally remember your physical looks depending on the way you carry it. Always ensure you love your body enough to sell your limitations as the next cool. Skinny bods seem to be the in-thing, however, you will take your seize fourteen body out nicely dressed with the right confidence and you will steal the show from the lady that has long legs with the shape of a bottle.

Something important to keep in mind is the fact that your physical looks may take you there but your depth of knowledge and ability to manage situations will sustain you there. Even beauty pageants test intelligence as part of the criterion for wining. Albeit Love yourself, rock the look that boosts your confidence, that is your first selling point.

I have learnt to appreciate nature and use it as my yardstick for measuring beauty, and I have even made it a type of therapy. I once lived in a beach house for about a year and I remember how I will walk to the beach whenever I feel down, admire the beauty of the water and the air that comes with the waves of the sea anytime I felt ill, I will do an hour or two watching the waves and exhaling and all the headache and fever will be gone before I leave the beach.

Beauty for me will always reside in moments created and memories deposited rather than mundane things acquired by money.

Love

I was brought up to understand that as a woman I had to hold myself in high esteem and that it was my responsibility to ensure that no man took advantage of me. No wonder I went through college and was never bold enough to have a relationship as I was too conscious of the need not to be taken advantage of by any man.

Love would be a sour topic for me to discuss at this point in my life especially with regards to relationships. My advice to everyone however, is to make love a decision not an unconscious adventure, in other words **I do not fall in love, love for me is a decision after consideration of a few factors.**

I would really love to come here and share my ideal views on love and how love should be perceived but unfortunately, whether directly or indirectly, love hasn't been exactly as straight forward as I read from Mills & Boons novels back then in primary school. The first time I had feelings for anyone, after three years of continuous chase and angelic composure by the person, the person had to end up in a dicey pregnancy scandal with his supposed X-wife, oh yes he had been married with a son before we met and when we met, I could tell that he was fighting several demons privately.

I accepted his hand of friendship mainly because I wanted to look in from a closer range, find out what the problem was and see if I could be a shoulder to lean on. He later opened up to me about struggling with separation from a violent marriage that failed and how he never thought he would one day be in that situation.

At this time, I was still trying to recover from the loss of my beloved sister who died in an abusive marriage and I vowed to be a voice of reason to save another human from losing themselves, their sanity or even their lives to an "unholy matrimony".

In his case, he was a youth pastor in his church and consequently a role model to the youth in his church where he served as a marriage counselor, how could he be found in that situation? He had managed to remain in it for that long because he didn't want anyone to know that he was struggling in his marriage but things later fell apart.

I bought him books and movies and tried my bit at counseling him and encouraging him to fight for his marriage and mend his broken home, I made it clear to him that I would never get intimate with him as I couldn't afford to be the reason why he was strong enough to leave his wife; little did I know that I would eventually get emotionally caught up. This person could have been the embodiment of a perfect example of a lover and a partner…he had the right words, the right attitude, the right looks and the right finance as well (lol) I could have sworn that the dedication was 110% until the bombshell dropped… oh yes there were fond memories, I remember travelling out of the country on official duties two days to my birthday and I remember the surprise and excitement when I got a call from "Mr. Right' informing me that he had flown down just to wish me happy birthday and spend the birthday night with me before hurrying to catch his 6am flight back home the following morning…I remember how everyday was valentine for us with the fond messages and surprise gifts rolling in, we bonded effortlessly and everyone that knew us knew that the chemistry was scientific (lol), his parents also started reaching out to me as I slowly got introduced to his family and him to mine.

My family wouldn't hear of it, how could I at barely 25yrs decide to be with a man who had been previously married? I stood up for him and protected him till my family gradually started accepting him after seeing that his heart was of gold and he meant well for me…before I begin to delve into memories that will only stay as memories, let's move on to the reality of what it is at the moment.

His attitude changed suddenly and it was clear that something was wrong, he had become distant and secretive; I remember the tears I cried and the pain when reality set in, his "X" was pregnant for him and he never told me until I found out, he told me there was an explanation but I refused to get involved in the explanation.

Badly enough when the next person came along, I was already too hurt and untrusting to open up, irrespective of how good his intentions were, I was unable to let go, I frustrated every effort he made to reach out to me and made him pay for the mistake of his predecessor.

Hmm Love…love is one concept I am still unable to understand or define, but I am convinced that I have felt love or at least I have felt a sincere connection to someone at some point. I am not sure if I am interested in another of those circles but I am certain that there were some of the most magical moments of my life.

Even the best of us get caught up in unbelievable love circles and love triangles but we must learn to not lose ourselves in the middle of these, just dust yourself up and love again.

Relationships

On relationships, I tell everyone: *No one is doing you a favor by being your friend or being with you, if there is no mutual respect and appreciation get out,* it is a "friendly-abuse" or a "relative-abuse" rather than a relationship. I have seen too many men and women lose themselves because they want to stay in a relationship. I have seen people become a shadow of themselves, go mental and even lose their lives like in the case of my late sister; and despite my strong Christian beliefs and foundation, I tell everyone that cares to listen, male and female alike; if it is not working, it is not working, please take the door. Separation is a great way of giving each other space to re-appreciate each other and either mend fences or realize it will never work and move on. Of course both parties must be willing to make compromises, think less about themselves and more about the other person and realize that no two individuals from different backgrounds and with different upbringings and life experiences will come together without having great differences but how you chose to handle your differences will determine the outcome of your relationship or union.

Never feel under pressure to be in a relationship, there is no trophy or reward for people who are constantly in one relationship or the other.

When I was in college, I had three friends and I was the youngest amongst all of us. I was constantly teased about my unchanging single status, I got used to it and after a while I could not be bothered anymore by their jokes and attempt to match-make me. I concluded that I was doing the right thing after having to console one of my friends each time one of her relationship fell apart despite her dedication and effort to keep it together.

The most interesting part of this was the fact that she seemed to feel obliged to get into another relationship as soon as the last one was done.

She ended up emotionally exhausted in no time and after a long conversation, we agreed that she should take a break and redefine what she wants from a relationship, what went wrong with the last one and what she could have done differently; this worked like magic and yours truly is currently married with two children to the man from that next relationship.

Again, it is important to check the motive behind

your relationship, why did you go into that relationship in the first place? Good looks? Money? Loneliness? Desperation to settle down? You need to be sure you are in the relationship for the right reasons, most importantly for reasons that will not fade easily otherwise the lifespan of the relationship is only as long as the reason you went into it in the first place.

Friends or Diamonds

Friends are a gift from God as mothers are God's blessing to an undeserving creation "mankind".

I will always choose friends over diamonds, even though you have not asked me why or how, I will tell you.

For me friendship is priceless and it is one of the best gifts that mankind received on earth. I have had friends that have become family and I have had friends that have made me wonder how God could have created such meanness out of man. I prefer to keep my circle closed and open up to a few people that I am comfortable with and I can trust but I like being surrounded by these selected few as much as possible.

I have had friends who have gone out of their way so much for me that I felt undeserving of such love. I remember arriving Dubai for one of my mother's routine health check-ups and calling my friend Dele who had invited us to stay with her in her apartment to save hotel bills and also give herself and myself the opportunity to catch up. Mum and I were at her place for about a week and throughout the period we were treated like royals, I had never experienced that much respect, love, courtesy and hospitality all my life and the effort she made to ensure that my mother was comfortable was incredible. I also remember a family friend giving me her school fees to pay as an advance for my abroad studies pending when funds come through from my parents and the best part of it was that I did not need to ask Omah, she offered by herself and gestures like that mean the most to me.

I have gone out of my way for friends in unexplainable ways as I am a firm believer of friendship. I remember accepting to go into an exam hall and impersonate my friend in order to help her write her exams because I was aware that she will not pass if she wrote the exam herself. Exam malpractice was totally against my ethics especially as a daughter of educationists, but the fear of leaving her behind was greater than the fear of being caught and expelled by the school authorities.

I have made crazier sacrifices for friends though, ah yes, I stayed back with my friend Joy to give her moral support amongst other things when she had extra papers to write after we graduated, would you believe that I walked into a lecturers office and told him that I know he made my friend to fail his exams because she did not give into his advances? Yes oh, "there is no way she would have had an F in your course while I had an A sir, I ensured that she copied everything I wrote because I knew that you would try to victimize her and your exams were objective not subjective sir", the lecturer looked at me in confusion, "what are you talking about?" he asked; "bring out her script and my script and let us compare sir, I am very sure about what I am saying and we can take it up to the school authorities". Yes I was that crazy, I walked up to a lecturer and admitted to exam malpractice just to save my friend from writing the exam again and guess what? That conversation lead to reconciliation between him and my friend and he eventually gave her a "c" and asked her not to re-write that paper.

    I have been betrayed severally by friends as well, I remember entering a lecturers office in college, and meeting my best friend at the time on her way out of his office. The lecturer explained to me that my friend had come to contest my grades, complaining that I had a distinction in the course while she had a "B". She complained to the lecturer that she was certain that there must be a mistake in the marking of the script because she was more prepared for the exam than I was and she advised that they check my script properly to be sure that I didn't deserve a "B" as well. It was a rude shock to me and I left the office that day asking myself questions but I decided never to speak to her about it.

I have tried to harden up and made up my mind to change my attitude towards friendship, but again a few friends have taught me how golden friendship can be.

My advice, don't stop loving and trusting simply because you have been betrayed in the past, if someone lets you go; it is their loss and not yours, new friends will come that will be your pillar and make you realize that friendship is precious; that is exactly the feeling I get when I speak with my "ride or die" Chiaka, she is so beautiful in her imperfections.

Sex

In this area I am not very savvy, as I have left this area quite underdeveloped and uncultivated. However, I believe sex is more than just a physical experience and should not be shared lightly. Of course I believe that sex should be left for marriage and shared with that unique partner.

Both parties should enjoy sex, it should actually be the act of a mutual effort to show love to one another, I think sex should be a short term mirror of what a relationship should be…give and take and sacrifices, each one trying to please the other and get one another to satisfaction. If one person gets an orgasm today it is the victory of the party who made it happen and vice-versa.

For me I am generally turned on by innocence, a man with self-control despite chemistry between us will always get my heart rather than a man who is loud and in a hurry to go to Jerusalem as soon as possible. It's quite irritating to me; what happened to being a gentleman and seeking my heart romantically till I can no longer resist you? I am of the old time religion and I am not ashamed to say that.

My word of advice for every woman though is that you keep your sex life very exciting for you and your husband, try out new things, tricks and locations and please do not be shy to demand satisfaction…there's absolutely nothing wrong with that, it's a two way trip, talk to each other about the highpoints and low points and help each other get better daily but in all, NEVER make sex the center of any relationship as that can only translate into a disaster and if you find that one person who satisfies you sexually and has a human face, don't let them go.

If you are a single lady, do not take sex trivially as the effects are numerous. You will feel used, broken and abandoned at the end of the day. If unwanted pregnancy occurs, you are left alone to go through the initial emotional trauma and stigma while the young man walks around freely.

If you contact a STDS, it is even worse as this may affect your fertility at the end of the day and several other issues may occur. Above all, I believe that there are deeper covenants that go with sex than just the 5mins of pleasure so have it with the right person only.

I believe in celibacy, if you are single and have an intending spouse, I think the excitement is more when you wait for marriage before sex, it does not matter if you are no longer a virgin, and celibacy shows a lot of physical discipline as well and also has its spiritual benefits.

Do not let anyone deceive you, there is nothing old fashioned about taking your stand and staying true to it.

Sex is better enjoyed in marriage.

Chapter 3:

My Entrepreneurial Journey...

Miss Independent's Lemon to Lemonade: I have always had a problem with having other people take care of my needs, hence my determination to work till my bones are weary and ensure that I can afford all my needs.

I've always said that my career chose me, I didn't choose it. I found myself doing all the things I do today without consciously working my way towards them. It's more like everything I did for fun, as a pastime or as passion came together and decided to develop into a career path for me, that is why I have never had to really work, I earn a living from living out my pass-time.

Everyone in my family including myself knew I was going to be a lawyer and take over my father's chambers, or so we thought; everyone knew I was a smart kid and I talked a lot so no doubt law was meant for me., I grew up looking at myself as a young lawyer in the making. I wrote JAMB and was a few points from the Law cut off score, I was very confident that my father will fix me up since he was well connected in the system but he declined stating that I was too young and should not be enabled.

I was registered to write Jamb a second time and I was thrown into Modern Languages and Translation Studies while waiting for my admission to Law and my squad was already so interesting that by the time my admission came through, I refused to move to Law despite all the threats from my parents, they were sure I was already on a path to failure because Modern Languages isn't a professional course.

In my fourth year, I had gone on holiday to my elder sister's house whose husband was a chartered accountant, we went to church on a Sunday and Pastor Paul Adefarasin preached about rejecting the mediocre life and reaching for the stars. To my dismay, my brother-in-law used me as a practical example of someone that is already set on the part to mediocrity; he finished by telling me "to finish wasting money on this first degree and go and get a proper degree". Determined to prove them wrong, I doubled my study efforts and graduated Best Student of my year which opened me up to a few opportunities.

Again, I also had this little thing going, I was the dance leader for the youth in my church. In College, I was always called to anchor departmental events and gatherings, when we had our final Award night…I remember anchoring full time and changing several outfits and getting loud ovations despite winning three Awards in total: Best Graduating Student, Contribution to departmental growth and social development, Most Social and Ethical Student…little did I know that this flare for socials and entertainment will later become my source of livelihood.

After our final exams, I travelled home to my family and after several family meetings, it was decided that I will be sent back to study law as soon as I was done with my NYSC. I wanted to study Law but I did not want to be sponsored by anyone having been told that my first degree was a waste.

I had to device a means of leaving home. I thought about different options and the opportunity finally presented itself when my dad wanted to travel to Calabar with his car. I pleaded with him that I needed to go with him so that I could help a close friend who my parents knew very well; she had carry over exams to write and also needed somewhere to stay for the short period. I explained that I needed to do revision with her to ensure that she is successful. My father agreed and we travelled.

I arrived Calabar same day as my friend, we prepared for the exams together, she wrote them and later informed me that she would love to stay back and search for a job as she did not want to go back home and stay idle, I told her I was in on the plan and we printed our CVs and started searching for jobs.

One week later, it was time to go home, my dad sent his driver to pick me but I escaped. That was the beginning of one of the toughest periods in my life. We soon ran out of food and money and had to embark on a compulsory fasting and prayer session for about a month, we will fast and pray till midday, eat our only meal for the day which was the left over Irish potatoes that my friend brought from Jos, we trekked from office to office, our nice shoes in our handbags and our trekking shoes on. When we arrived any office, we took off our trekking-shoes by the gate and wore our nice high-heel shoes and walked in with a smile to submit our CVs. I was eventually given an ultimatum to return home. We submitted our CVs to two places before I left, one was a referral from a friend and the other one was a referral from my department as Best Graduating Student.

I travelled back home and my mum informed me that she was travelling to Ghana and she wanted me to accompany her and stop in Lagos to baby seat my niece in Lagos till it is time for NYSC. I broke down totally, I was not going to justify their assertion that my first degree was a waste of finances especially since the niece in question was the daughter of my in-law who had labeled me a mediocre. I cried silently to God in my heart.

A day to the famous trip, I received a call, I had been offered employment with the prestigious KORA All African Music Awards, my resumption date will be communicated later. I told my mum and she said I will go to Lagos and stay baby seating till it was resumption time. I cringed inside me but I did not feel too bad since I knew redemption was near. The following day, I received another call and I had been offered employment with Tinapa Resorts as part of the organizers of the Launch and 1st Tinapa International Trade Expo and I was to resume immediately, what was even better was the fact that I was considered for both jobs because of my language prowess. I was over the moon with excitement. I knew my liberation had come and everyone knew I was unstoppable. I parked my bag and headed back to Calabar to resume work immediately. And even when I was given my contract with KORA Awards, I attempted to run both jobs concurrently till the demands became too high and I could no longer manage both jobs.

When I left college and got introduced to my first and second jobs, both jobs initially seemed language based since I was multilingual, it was an opportunity for me to prove to my family that my chosen field was not as useless as they thought. *I however applied myself on the job till I found other ways of being useful and both jobs turned out to be entertainment jobs. I worked extra hours, took initiative, made sure I delivered given tasks within deadlines, offered myself when an extra hand was needed in other departments' e.t.c I knew I had to learn as much as possible and the top was my target so I put in the work.*

I was quick to realize that God had already destined my path and I would never really succeed if I diverted.

It hasn't been rosy all through. Being a female in the entertainment industry and having youngish looks do not go hand in hand with being a moralist whose mama taught that principles should be respected. I have had to forgo jobs, correct impressions, make sacrifices, act a part that I am not e.t.c to keep it going without losing my mind and the only way it was possible to hold on was because I was doing something I actually love to do…remind me again why I counsel people with the famous quote "chose a career that you love and you will never have to work a day"

Despite the set-backs encountered when I left KORA and the attempts by my X-boss at the time to obstruct most of my solo projects, I am thankful for the grace to have taken certain decisions at the right time as those decisions taken at that time set me on a path that literarily defined my career today and what I stand for.

I have learnt to see the light socket in every situation, and seek to switch the light on rather than cry about the darkness.

Young & Naïve:

For me, my break into KORA All African Music Awards was like my dream job finding me. I was very young when I joined KORA, about 19years old. Initially I was recruited as a bilingual phone operator taking enquiries from artistes from all over the world speaking English, French and Spanish, I remember receiving a call from 2face Idibia, just after African Queen...Lord, I felt I had arrived. I was later trained to present the prestigious Red Carpet for KORA Awards, it was like a dream come through. It was a lot for me at that age as I was quickly introduced to the crème-de-la-crème of the society and the industry. It quickly became life on the fast lane flying from one country to another, flying business class, keeping up appearances, trying to live up to public expectations e.t.c. Of course it was very exciting at the beginning, we were received by presidents in some countries and my official car will have a presidential plate-number driving in a convoy and all...I felt I had blown...lol.

On the other hand, my family was worried about me because I was supposed to go for a 2nd degree in Law, as far as they were concerned, entertainment was a waste of time, it was for unintelligent people and miscreants. I always tried to send gifts home to create an impression that I was on top of money in order for my family to leave me alone, I also had to take up online courses and send my results and certificates home to satisfy my family.

One remarkable lesson I learnt from mixing with celebrities from different cultures and high flying political officials is the fact that "A woman needs to keep herself, respect herself and maintain dignity and self-respect" as I was privy to several conversations where women were explained off in the most disrespectful manner simply because they compromised their integrity for material gifts.

On the other hand, I never lost sight of the fact that I am my mother's daughter, I doubled up as personal assistant to the KORA president and that was the sour part, I worked so hard behind the scenes, I slept for 3hours at most. so much work keeping the team together and cleaning up the mess behind my boss (I guess that is where I learnt a lot about PR and diplomacy), the irritating part which I have never mentioned all these years was the fact that my boss started making advances at me, at first I was terribly shocked because he paraded himself like a moralist so I could not understand this new discovery...in fact, he attempted to rape me twice & I could not understand why me; because I knew he could get almost any girl he wanted.

I had just finished collating the result of the jury for KORA 2008 for which I was kept in isolation in a hotel room with my phones switched off for 3days to avoid external interference, I called my bosses room number and informed him that I had finally finished and he asked me to come to his hotel room with the score sheets, when I arrived his room, the door opened to a dark room with a pot-belled man in only a small pair of shorts. I looked closely and that was my boss, with his arms wide open asking me to give him a hug...I was not quite sure why he was half naked, he knew I was coming to his room (I thought, feeling quite confused). As for the hug, I convinced myself he wanted to encourage my hard work and that must be part of being civilized right? I timidly walked towards him and stood in front of him, and he hugged really tightly and said "let us go to the bed" I was no longer confused, I was pretty sure of what I heard, I told him I didn't want to go to his bed and I would rather go to my room. I had just come to handover the results from the jury. Things started going quickly, he pushed me to the bed and started telling me how 99% of men in the world were sleeping with their assistants and it is no news. I struggled and pleaded with him as he kept trying to pull down my jean. "Please sir, I am a virgin, please I don't want to do this sir" his response was very *comforting* "I will be gentle with you, I will not penetrate properly", he kept trying to convince me,

Then the door opened slightly, and he quickly let go.

Apparently I didn't shut the door properly when I entered his room and I had also called our Nigerian representative on the phone and asked him to meet me in my boss's room so that we could go through the result, he came and knocked and noticed that the door was not properly locked so he tugged at the door and it gave way...Isn't my God a good God?

The following day was supposed to be a busy one, we had a technical team that had just arrived from South Africa and of course we had some site recce to do as well as long production meetings and I was to coordinate everything, I handled my duties nonchalantly all day because I was not sure I still wanted to work, I felt betrayed.

My boss arrived and found out that a lot of things weren't in place, he sent for me and as he was about to begin questioning me, I told him we needed to have an urgent conversation before anything else. I explained to him how upset I was at the event of the previous day, I told him that he had a right to assigning duties to his staff and I have a right to decide what type of job I could handle, "if sleeping with you is one of the duties of your PA, I would rather resign as I won't do it; I neither have ailing parents or children to cater to, I would rather go home to my family" I said. He was shocked at my guts and he told me we will talk about it later.

A few days later, I was called into a meeting with two of my senior colleagues and their salaries were reviewed upwards while I was told that I am a risk to the company as I had the potential to destroy the name of the company quickly and my services would be terminated. I smiled, picked up my bag and said thank you...off I went without any regrets.

My boss called me two weeks later and started singing my praises, he was proud of me and he had only tested me to be sure that his opponents and friends would not be able to access me sexually and use gifts to win over information from me. He was proud of how morally upright I was and my job had been restored immediately with an upward review in my salary. I was over the moon with excitement, I mean I was less than 20 years and I was quite **naïve** at the time.

RAPE, POISON & RESIGNATION

Then it happened again about 2years later, it actually happened twice in quick succession and I told myself it was time to move on, the 2nd time was very scary and annoying. We were in the middle of planning the 20th anniversary of African Music, it was quite a hectic time as I was charged with the responsibility of liaising with our major sponsor, liaising with the technical team from south Africa, keeping the entire team up to speed, coordinating Akons arrival and logistics and getting our equipment out of Burkina Faso where the equipment was stuck because my boss had fallen out with the number 2 man of the country before we left Burkina Faso, and the number 2 man was the one that facilitated the arrival of the aircraft with the equipment and had all the documents.

I worked literarily round the clock, and on this particular day, after we closed from work by 10pm, my boss and I proceeded for a meeting with one of our sponsors and that meeting was on till about 2am, major discussions were done but the "big boys" were just chatting away so I went to my boss and asked him if I could leave since we always moved around in two different cars; he agreed and I left back to our apartment which we had rented, I stayed downstairs while my boss stayed upstairs and we had an office within the apartment where the staff resumed and we worked from there.

I got into my room and proceeded to lock the door from inside as usual but noticed that there was a problem with the lock; I made a mental note to ask the house keeper to fix it in the morning. I changed up and tied my towel with the intention of taking a shower and running off to bed but tired as I was, I decided to rest for five minutes on my bed before going to the bathroom and that was how I slept off.

The feeling of human presence in my room woke me up about an hour later, I opened my eyes to a dark room (I always slept with my lights on by the way), I tried to look around the dark room without making it obvious that I was consciously awake, there he was; my boss, stripped, from head to toe without a piece of clothing on him, carefully moving towards me, my head did a 360 trying to decide what to do, remember I had only a towel wrapped around me with no under wears, NOTHING, he quickly got to the bed and started trying to caress my laps, I held his hand and said stop this Ernest, stop this please, I was emotionally drained, physically tired and generally frustrated, I felt helpless.

Screaming will be useless as it was such a big house, besides did I expect the cook or house keeper to run in from the boys quarters to save me from their boss? Struggling ensued and things were moving really fast, my towel was almost on the floor and the beast had succeeded in pinning one of my legs down, I remember saying to him that if he succeeded with his intentions, one of us will not leave that room alive "and that person will not be me" he paused and looked at me for a minute and said the most stupid thing I had heard in my entire life "Victoria I'm in love with you, haven't you realized that by now? Let's do this and I will treat you right. I will marry you if you want" he said progressing with his wrinkled penis towards my privates, I decided to buy time by engaging him in a conversation "I care about you too sir, but this is not how to show it, I have fantasized about my first sex experience, I would like it to be very romantic and somewhere on an Island, can we not plan to travel somewhere after this event and do all these? I kept blabbing but noticed he was progressing quickly. "Okay let me just rub it around a bit, I won't go inn too deep" Rub what where? I thought to myself, PENIS??? No ways Victoria, I thought in anger, flashes of fire and brimstone and strength from nowhere, I pushed him off the bed, he fell on the floor and I jumped out of bed quickly, albeit without my towel. I moved out of the apartment very early the next morning, checked into a hotel and kept convincing myself to stay and finish the Akon concert like a professional.

I booked my ticket and flew back to Nigeria without his knowledge immediately after the post production was done , I ruminated a bit about my next steps and went ahead to dust the documents for my company that I had registered. I put together the little funds that I had as well and started planning a TV reality show. I already had a few people that were indirectly part of my team so we started putting together proposals and scripts and searching for sponsors, locations e.t.c

POISON

Exactly one month before the Akon concert, I got on a plane and flew to Burkina Faso to arrange for our equipment to be moved to Benin Republic. Ahead of my arrival, the younger sister of the first lady of Burkina Faso had gotten in touch with me and requested that we see when I get into town; she wanted to speak with me about learning a thing or two on Events Production. I figured that I would need her help to unravel the mystery around those equipment, after all she was part of the "first family" and she lived in the villa.

She came to my hotel and we had lunch and she planned to take me shopping the next day e.t.c, our friendship grew and she became my confidant and help, taking me to meet the people that could facilitate the release of the equipment including the number 2 man who my boss had offended. In fact she opened up to me that he was asking her out and I felt that was good bait to use in getting the man's support.

I kept turning in circles as each time I felt closer to getting the approval to move the equipment, something will happen and things will be back to where I started. I was not feeling very happy on this day and my friend had come to take me out. We went and did some shopping (everyone who knows me well knows that shopping is one of my most efficient therapies). We got back to my hotel around midday and I insisted we have lunch together at the hotel. We ordered lunch at the hotel restaurant, I just couldn't understand the vibes that I was getting from her and the waiter but I felt something was off. We later parted ways and planned to reconvene later that evening. She had promised to speak to her sister "The First Lady" to see how she could intervene. I sat at the pool side of my hotel wondering what to do, I reached out to the best friend of the president who had wanted us to be "friends with benefits" while I was in the country, I also reached out to the Technical Assistant of the Minister of Transport and Infrastructure" he was the second most powerful man in the country and no thanks to my boss's erratic nature, we were not in his good books. I was lost in thought when I felt someone seat next to me and touched my shoulders, this good looking American middle aged guy was trying so hard to make a conversation, he eventually borrowed my phone charger and gave me his phone number and room number.

My phone rang and it was my friend, "on va diner au villa ce soir, je te prends a 18heure" she said (we will have dinner at the villa this evening, I will pick you up by 6pm), She picked me up, stopped by her boyfriend's house and then to the villa. Everywhere seemed quiet when we got in, she chatted a bit and she asked the chef to serve our food after which we will meet the first lady. My name was labeled on my plate and her plate was plain, we started eating and half way through, she received a text message and had to hurriedly drop me off at my hotel, I was a bit disappointed but I did not want to be over bearing. I got into my hotel room at about 10:30pm and slept off in disappointment, I woke up at 12:30am with a sharp pain in my stomach, the pain was increasing quickly and spreading around my lower abdomen, then I started to throw-up. I was sweating profusely, I struggled to my table and picked up the large bottle of water and started drinking, the circle continued, drink and throw up even more.

I was getting very weak, I reached out for my phone and started calling the American who had borrowed my charger earlier in the day, and then I sent him a text message with my room number saying I need to be taken to the hospital urgently. Things got worse, I started stooling as well and I could swear that my intestines were melting. I had finished the bottle of water by then and I rolled on the floor till I got to the restroom, struggled to seat on the toilet while drinking water from the tap in the rest room. I was stooling and vomiting and probably dying while trying to think of how to get help.

I rolled back to the room and texted the Technical Assistant to the Minister of Transport and Infrastructure and he responded immediately and he showed up at my hotel door and opened the room with the help of the reception. Well I remembered waking up the next day to a message from Valerie (The Technical Assistant to the Minister) that read "your equipment will be ready to move by tomorrow, you need to leave Burkina immediately, you were poisoned". I booked my ticket, I did not want to hear story, my parents had lost a daughter already, and I wasn't going to put them through the same pain for a second time in such quick succession.

QTABY EVENTS

In less than a year after leaving KORA, I had exhausted my savings without getting any confirmed sponsor for my TV reality show. Back to square one with just my car and barely enough money to feed at the time, I reached out to my parents for support and as expected they asked me to come back home. My mum said "whatever you are doing out there, if it is not working anymore, comeback home". My dad eventually sent money for my air ticket which I converted into survival funds while I tried to offer my services to a presidential candidate in one of the francophone countries for his rally, I got paid and started building a client base.

It was a quick lesson for me as I realized the importance of starting slowly and giving yourself a chance to grow as opposed to jumping the gun and trying to do more than you can at once.

I also learnt some hard facts and business principles: you must find the diamond in the roughness; in your seeming bad situation lies a lot of opportunities.

I received an email from one of the organizations that worked with us on Projects and Logistics while I was with KORA asking if I will be available to handle their liaison in Nigeria, of course I agreed and they gave me my first major deal. I ensured the project was handled with a high level of professionalism and found my way to their heart.

My company became their liaison around West Africa and we handled major high profile events with them. Along the line, I started getting contacted by artistes that I had met and dealt with during my sojourn at KORA Awards, they needed me to either help them get collaboration with another artiste or handle promotion for them. I eventually decided to do Artiste Management professionally and this metamorphosed to Talent Management. We thought about the best way to get slots for our talents in events and we decided to put to use our skill and knowledge of Events Production. We progressed slowly but steadily, we got to produce some of the most prestigious events in the country like The Headies Awards, AFRIMA e.t.c for brands; we also started producing our own events like Cruisenchillz boat cruise event and TV contents like Captain English and Olajumoke Sauce.

Qtaby Events has since evolved to become a household name in the industry, going through phases of glory and difficult times. Most importantly, we are making a difference, and impacting society. One important advise for entrepreneurs, ensure you sell the vision to your team as you will need them to keep the vision alive at some point and in all you do "Get your company a Jimi". Qtaby Events story will never be complete without adding the contribution of the star who bought the vision from me and totally ran with it, it does not matter that I watched him grow from a young inexperienced boy into the Boy In Total Control of Himself that he now is.

While I would like to tell you that your dreams are valid, while I would like to motivate you with hope speeches, I will also like to remind you to believe in the process, it takes time to build a solid brand that will stand the test of time. Always remember who you are and do not compromise who you are for immediate aggrandizement. The long run is far more important than the now.

DRAMA

This book will not be complete if I do not let you a bit into the kind of drama that I deal with managing talents and how priceless it is to have gained enough experience on the job to help carry me through.

My company was contracted by MTN Benin to do Artiste Booking and Talent Management for its yearly summer beach event called "Yellow Summer". We contracted Wizkid as one of the artistes and he travelled with his team of about seven people including his heartthrob at the time; Tania Omotayo. We arrived Benin Republic and I was quite impressed at his work ethics, he created a studio out of one of the rooms as soon as he arrived and immediately started recording with his producers who accompanied him on the trip.

When it was eventually show time, we had made provisions for enough cars for the team only to realize that one of his friends who came to join him in the hotel came with two "female groupies" and wanted to get them in the car thereby taking up space for relevant team members. My logistics manager politely asked the girls to get off the car for the crew to go, he however promised them that one of the drivers will come back to the hotel to pick them up after dropping the team.

Wizkid was apparently unhappy with this decision and planned to get back at us unknown to us. After the performance, there was an after party with the sponsors at the club which was scheduled to take place at midnight; and even though the contract that was signed with Wizkid and his team stated that he was contractually bound to participate in both events, he went incommunicado when it was time for the after party.

I was feverish because I had just arrived from a 6hours flight and continued by road to Cotonou for this event, I woke up from sleep at about 11:45pm and called my Logistics Manager to confirm if they were already on their way to the after party, he explained to me that he was with Wizkids manager in front of Wizkids room but he was not responding to calls on his mobile phone as well as his room phone and they had been trying to reach him for close to an hour. I thought a bit about what to do and I walked to the front of his room and behold the two of them were seated in front of his room trying to figure out what to do.

I immediately asked Jimi to run to the reception and ask them to come and open the door with the master key, I feigned concern and distress at the same time. I accused the manager of being irresponsible, I said "your talent is locked up in a room and not responding to phone calls, what if something terrible has happened to him in that room? What if he is in some sort of trouble?

How can both of you sit down here? We need to open the door and be sure that all is well with him, this has nothing to do with my event, this is about his life and safety. Jimi run down and get someone from the reception to open the door right away" I spoke in a very loud voice because my intention was for Wizkid to hear what I said from inside his room and know that he needed to come out or else his room will be opened either ways.

It worked like magic. Less than 2mins after I spoke, Wizkid called his managers mobile phone and said "you guys should calm down na, I will be out in 5 minutes" I smiled inwardly and when he came out he said "mama go and rest and let the boys handle this na, you look tired, we will be okay". Of course I had achieved my objective as I did not want to be found wanting by my client MTN. I thanked him for his concern and did a dramatic sign of the cross thanking God that he was okay.

Wizkid is a sweet soul to work with by the way so this is not an attempt to show grievance, it is just the reality of what my job entails and I will probably not be paid if things were otherwise.

If I go back to details of my first working

experience with Nigerian Pop Singer Davido, you will realize that the drama with WIzkid was even a child's play as Davids episode can be produced into a full blown comedy series.

David was also contracted for one of the Yellow Summer Events, I met with his Manager Kamal, we signed a contract and an advance was paid, unknown to me Asa Asika was still taking bookings for Davido and that became an entirely different episode as Asa made a conflicting booking that we were able to resolve eventually. Since I was travelling, I gave Davidos balance to a mutual friend of Kamal and myself to pay to them the Friday before their departure and that was the beginning of my nightmare...I was to get back to Lagos on Thursday and leave to Cotonou with David and his team on Saturday morning.

I called my friend who I gave the balance to and his phone numbers were switched off, I sent a message and he replied telling me he was in America; that was the last I heard from him.

I reached out to Davids manager only to realize that my friend did not pay Davids Manager the balance. It was 3pm on Friday afternoon already and I had to mop up N2,000 000 to pay David his balance as our contract said full payment before departure.

After a lot of calls and using all my ATM cards, I was able to withdraw about N1,750 000. Kamal and I agreed that the money will be handed to them in cash before departure; we agreed to leave Lagos by 6am on Saturday as we were travelling by road and needed to arrive on time for signing of autographs. I started calling Davido and his manager from 5:30am till 8am before Kamal picked his call and asked that we meet by 11am at the national stadium, I was livid. I did some intelligence gathering and realized that they had actually travelled to Abuja for an event the previous night and they had also taken a booking for a performance for mid-day on Saturday at the national stadium despite being contractually bound to do autograph signing in Cotonou by midday of the same day; meanwhile I had sent the vehicles that we hired for the project to Davids house by 5am that morning.

I started making my way to the stadium by 9am, I arrived there and met with the organizers of the stadium event, pleaded with them to make Davids performance the first instead of the last and explained the situation to them. They were surprised to realize that David was in Abuja as well. They eventually obliged my request and put Davidos performance as the first performance for the day. Things got very intense when I called the airport and realized that the flight that they were to travel on had been delayed by two hours.

I called Kamal and told him their flight had been

delayed and he asked me "flight from where?" so I explained to him that I was aware that he was in Abuja and he also has a performance in Lagos...he tried to deny at first and he eventually spoke the truth when he realized that I had all the details.

They finally arrived Lagos and were on their way from the airport to the stadium when I got a call from the company that rented cars to us for the trip, they informed us that they were no longer willing to make the trip as the scheduled time for the trip was 6am and at 1pm we were yet to leave, they were also unwilling to refund the advance that we had paid them.

Damage control again: getting 3 SUVs to make the road trip at that time, finding extra funds to pay for the cars considering the fact that all the cash I had mopped up was to pay the artist balance before the trip and I was still a few hundreds of thousands short. On the other hand I had the MTN agency in Benin Republic calling me every 10mins because they were worried that Davido would not show up and their image was at stake.

We were eventually able to manage the situation, he arrived, did his performance and was obliged to use one of his personal cars to make the road trip while my car served as the second car and I was able to hire one extra car which was not an SUV, Davido explained that he needed to get to his house to pick up a few documents and international passport but I would not hear of it. I paid the balance and explained that the N250,000 will be sorted on arrival in Cotonou...we managed to get ourselves to Cotonou and had the event amidst several other melodramatic occurrences in the course of the trip and I eventually had to leave them in the country, an act which caused another round of drama. I however recognized a huge potential in Davido through that project, he ultimately had the right attitude.

Dealing with drama like this one is a part of my job and the skills and ability to resolve and make sense of issues like this is actually part of what the brands pay for when they pay us to handle artist bookings for them.

Chapter 4:

Purpose, Gifts & Miracles...

I realized from an early age that I had a purpose and that I was not born to be regular or ordinary. I realized early that I was called unto greatness and greater purposes than I could understand.

I had special abilities that were beyond me even as a child and I grew up to realize that I must fulfill the purpose for which all of these gifts were deposited in me.

As a child, I could read people's minds, this may sound weird but it is true and it almost became a burden to me. I remember seating next to my mum one morning when an uncle came to visit my mum with a business proposal that required that my mum gives him about half a million as far back as 1992.

He kept telling my mum about all the good intentions and prospects of the business. I sat there and his thoughts flashed before me like a video and I could see at every point that what he was saying was different from his actual intentions. He was actually silently praying for my mother to release the funds so that he could build a house on the land that he had acquired. I sat there with my mouth open and as soon as he stepped out I told my mum exactly what I had seen...she looked at me and smiled and concluded that I was just imagining. Alas she signed the document and paid him a first advance and that was the last time that she heard from him. A few other occurrences and my parents started respecting my suggestions.

A few years later, I lost that divine gift but the memories of those beautiful moments stayed with me.

Miracles

I have also benefitted from a number of miracles in my life that convinced me again that I could not afford to stray from whatever purpose God created me to serve.

The examples are countless but I will share a few.

When I was to go for my National Youth Service, I had to take permission from my boss since I was working already. I was given one day permission to go to camp so I went and did a preliminary registration and ran back to Lagos since I had a production meeting that I was to coordinate the next day.

Things got very busy and I could not resume back to camp within the three days given before camp arrivals closed. My friend had called me from camp and told me not to bother coming as they had concluded the headcount but my sister Lilly urged me to go and give it a try. I prayed and I managed to return back the day after the camp closed. I was advised to see the camp commandant before parade starts the next morning so I made my way to the front of the camp commandant's house. I saw a young man standing there as well and I approached him to ask some questions.

I later found out that he had done his complete registration but he only came to camp with the photocopy of his "call-off-letter" and had asked his parents to courier the original copy which had gotten missing in transit. The camp Director had given him that day as the last day to produce his original letter or go home.

I joined him to the Camp Directors house as advised and I presented my case to the Director. The Director listened to me and asked me to hold on. He then requested for the original copy of the young man's letter and he explained again that the letter was yet to arrive. The Director took my documents and told me that I was God sent to get him out of trouble as he had done the head count and included the boy as the last number on the camp and he needed to send all original documents and could not produce the complete number of documents to match the number he had declared to the headquarters in Abuja and he was already a day late. He advised the boy to return home and defer his Youth Service to the next badge and gave me the slot that he had reserved for the boy. I broke down in tears as I felt responsible for the boys predicament, I told the Director I will go home and I started pleading on the boys behalf. The Director was surprised and he asked if I was not the same person begging to be accepted a few minutes ago.

The boy held my hand and said "I was probably sent to camp to reserve this space for you, I am glad that God used me to stand in for you. You are a special person Victoria, do not feel bad"…I realized immediately that he was my angel, sent to stand in for me while I could not be there.

I have had several other similar experiences and I marvel each time at the way things fall into place for me once I pray and make a little effort.

As a university undergraduate I was very smallish but known to be a force to reckon with in my department. We had a new Spanish lecturer who had a particularly disturbing habit of announcing tests in the morning and mandating all students to buy his handouts on the same day before writing the test.

Mr. Luyen was known for several other unpalatable escapades, one day he came to class and threatened the entire class and I mobilized our class representative and we both went to Mr. Luyen's office. I spoke first "good day sir, we have come to tell you that the test you scheduled for today cannot happen because you have not taught us anything, you also cannot expect us to buy the handouts you informed us about this morning ahead of a 4pm test today as we did not leave our homes carrying that kind of money with us".

He asked me to leave his office and I obliged but before leaving I said "You do not know how to teach, you come into the class each time and stand by the board talking to yourself and leave without passing anything across, your pronunciations are also incorrect, you need to reconsider your methods as you are being paid to teach us and not to make our lives difficult". When I left his office, I realized I had overdone myself and so I went straight to the Head of Department to discuss the issue, while speaking to the HOD, the same lecturer I was reporting walked in and sat down and listened to my report, I could not stop as I knew I had been caught already. I made my report and also informed the HOD that the said lecturer threatens students that that refuse to give into his sexual advances. I knew that I had drawn a battle line when I left the HOD's office, I went to class wondering what to do next and when Mr. Luyen came to class later, he pointed me out and warned me not to let him take my matriculation number down as he would ensure I stay back 4 years after my colleagues graduated. I stood up and read out my matriculation number to him and assured him that he could do nothing to me.

I went home that night and I just could not sleep. I got on my knees and begged God to intervene "I said Lord I know I over did it, I am sorry but please take control and do not let me suffer for my lack of control".

The following day, Mr. Luyen came to class very early and addressed the entire class on how unserious we were and at the end of his speech he said "there is only one serious student in this class, her name is Victoria Nkong; that girl will have a distinction in my course no matter what happens, she is focused, dedicated to her work and extremely intelligent"...everyone starred in surprise, questions from all over started pouring in after he left the class "what did you do Victoria? How did the sudden change happen? What happened between yesterday and today?" I had no explanation myself, I smiled and told them I had a word with my Father in Heaven and my Heavenly Father spoke to him.

I could go on and on with the many miracles in my life, one of such experiences will be found in the story behind the orphanage which I will share below.

My Most Precious Gift (Life Fountain)

I come from a modest Christian family with predominantly female siblings. All my siblings were serving in church at different levels especially my sisters who were all in the choir, they will come home singing together after choir rehearsals and as soon as I attempted to join them to sing everyone will burst out laughing, they all said my voice wasn't good. I quietly started asking God how he will want me to serve him, what I could do for his kingdom e.t.c. As I became a teenager, I realized that I derived joy from putting a smile on other people's faces, solving their problems even to my detriment and even when it was not convenient for me.

Again with my parents open door nature, we got to feed a lot of people that were not part of my family and my mother made it clear to us that no child deserves to go hungry. I started taking particular interest in kids on the street begging for food and kids from extremely disadvantaged homes. I decided that when I grow up I would open an "open kitchen" where less privileged children on the streets were guaranteed two meals daily.

This dream changed when I lost my elder sister to domestic violence in 2010 and her husband eloped with her kids. I started visiting orphanage homes on weekends and generally learning about child care.

I was wounded; I returned to my goal to start a charity at 25 years old, but decided to make it an orphanage home where motherless children can have a family and proper care. I was making my plans with baby steps when I met the chairman of Japaul, I had been called for an interview for a bilingual position in Japaul Oil and Maritime Services Limited, I attended the interview with little or no interest and during my interview/chat session with the Japaul chairman I informed him that even if I got the job I would not be there for more than 6months as I was working on other projects. He wanted to know what projects and I told him about my company which I had put on hold after my sisters demise and that I was working on opening an orphanage home, he eventually indicated interest and decided to set up an orphanage home, he told me he will take the journey with me. I was super excited and this happened when I was exactly 25.

We quickly registered the foundation, then found out we needed to register an orphanage home, we did that and were told that we need to register officially with Lagos State Government. That later proved to be the toughest part of the registration process. We finally surpassed all the challenges and in April 2013 our first set of children were brought to us by the government.

The home kicked off and as it grew I had my experiences which helped me discover some qualities I had which had been redundant. I slowly became the mother to the children at the home as our objective was to give the children a sense of belonging and a setting as close as possible to a normal family. I learnt a lot about loving regardless from my children. The unconditional love they show me daily and their ability to trust me totally even when I am tricking them.

Five years later, the orphanage has become a blessing as it has proven in my lowest moments to be my source of strength and the most precious gift that life could have given me.

There has been happy moments, we have had successes reuniting some children with their biological parents, we have also had remarkable success finding parents to adopt some of the children. There has been "trying times" as well as sad moments. I have fought battles to save the life of my children, we have had several success stories and I have also lost a child in the most dramatic circumstance, this was a very painful experience and I do not wish any human being suffers such pain.

Baby Kunle was one of my biggest success stories at the orphanage. Baby Kunle and his sister were found at a refuse dump and they had all been injected with an overdose of drugs. He was 3months old while his sister was about 4years old. On arrival, we took Kunle for preliminary checkup and the doctor said we could take him home, there was something weird about his skin texture and color but since the doctor said he was okay, we brought him home.

Later that night Kunle started stooling and vomiting and we did three trips to the hospital between 11pm and 2am. We were later referred to another hospital by the doctor who realized that the situation was beyond him. The hospital we were referred to could not attend to him because their ward was full so there was no bed space, as much as I pleaded, they would not listen so I was back on the road again with baby Kunle. My driver was not resident at the home so I was driving round Lagos with a sick child in the car threatening to give up on me with his weak breath. I kept praying as I drove through Lagos by 3:30am. I finally located a pediatric hospital that someone had mentioned to me a while back. The doctor picked Kunle up from my hand and ran upstairs, drip lines, oral medications and injections at once.

We battled his life from 4am to 3:30pm later that afternoon before he stabilized. It was only after he became stable that I remembered that I was supposed to submit my dissertation for my MBA by 12noon that day, I had missed the deadline and of course there were corresponding consequences.

Kunle grew up to become the cutest baby I ever met with a smile that seemed to say "everything will be alright" as his smile had an unusual soothing effect.

His father eventually showed up and he was reunited with his family even though he cried for several days after he went home as he missed the home he had found with us.

Charity has also become a big part of my life as I have curated and managed several charity projects for the foundation. Outreach to slums and outreach to widows.

If we want to create a society that is bearable for all of us, we need to create a better place for the people who are in danger of growing up to create problems in the society. In all of these, I have learnt that the most rewarding activities in life are activities which are dedicated to helping others as we rise by lifting others.

Chapter 5:

My Realities...

There is a popular saying that "the grass is always greener on the other side" this notion has actually gotten a lot of people into trouble and even depression. We tend to admire all that we see and hear about other people and forget to celebrate ourselves for all that we are and how far we have come.

I got to realize early in life that things are not always the way they seem. You spend time envying what another person has and wishing it belonged to you, while the other person is looking at your life and seeing perfection.

The first step to wining in life is actually accepting your reality, "Pain or Gain"; and actually coming to terms with the fact that nothing last forever.

Pain, Prejudice, Challenges, Shame & Winning

Prejudice

Oh how I hate to be judged and oh how much I have gotten used to being misjudged. It has however taught me to not judge because appearance could be deceitful and looks could be misleading as well, things are never really the way they seem. Anyways, didn't the holy book itself admonish us to "judge not so that we be not judged"?

How often does a headline in the dailies actually mirror the true content of the news or interview that it is introducing? How many times has a book been judged by its cover only to realize that it was a wrong bound or meant to be a source of suspense?

Due to my personality and the industry that I operate in, I know how many times I have been wrongly judged at first site, it is one of the most constant occurrences in my life.

I remember working in an office where they had a routine of praying as a team every morning with one staff leading the prayers. The list for staff to lead prayers was released and all staff names except mine was on the list; I asked the HR why my name was omitted and he answered bluntly that from looking at me it can be easily deduced that I do not know how to pray.

I also remember judging a few people wrongly and even being caught in the act on a few occasions before deciding to always look closely and never judge.

We had this concert with Akon in Benin Republic, and Akon arrived with his crew. I was the one managing and coordinating the negotiations and production details so naturally I was at the airport to welcome him with my team. I collected all the crew passports and gave to my hostesses to fill their airport arrival forms. Akons uncle Alioune, who doubles as his road manager kept asking and demanding that I return the passports and I got irritated and felt already that he was being overbearing like most artistes managers that I know. I also concluded that he could have only gotten the position of Akon's road manager because of his family ties with Akon. I made an unkind comment about him in French to my assistant with the believe that he spoke only English and he instantly replied in French explaining nicely to me that they had an experience recently where a crew members' passport was misplaced under similar circumstances; he also apologized for any inconveniences he had caused by asking for the passport. I have never felt more guilty especially because in the days that followed, Alioune proved to be the most mature, professional and understanding of Akon's crew and one of the best artist managers that I have met.

I have since learnt to give benefit of doubts until I

am proven wrong, this also comes with its inconveniences but I rather err on the path of caution especially because I would love to be treated in the same way.

Pain

Pain for me could be translated to a state of mind when an expectation has been cut short due to a loss, a betrayal of trust, an expectation that didn't come through e.t.c. Being an extremely emotional person, I have successfully built a wall around me to protect myself from giving in easily to friendships and expecting too much from people so that I don't end up hurt too often. However, when I eventually open up to anyone, the pain I feel by a betrayal from the person is almost life threatening.

The most painful occurrence in my life would be the loss of my elder sister, no pain so far can be compared to the pain that I felt at that time. It was a phase in my life that eventually defined the rest of my life.

Lilly and I were staying together in the two bedroom flat that had been rented for us by my parents while I rounded up my final year in school and she worked with Addax Oil and we both managed her boutique off campus. The entire family knew the man she was going to get married to as he was no stranger to any of us.

Then I noticed this long phone calls that she started making every evening, I eavesdropped a couple of times and eventually realized that there was a new man in her life, it didn't make any sense to me; where was Uncle Jay? What was going on?

Fast forward three months later she was married to this "weird" man who the entire family had kicked against but she was adamant and claimed that she was in love; I recall vividly how I went into my mums room on the day of Lilly's "Marriage Introduction" and found my mum crying.

I asked mum what was wrong and she said "I just feel there is something terribly wrong with this man and the urgency with which they are getting married" I called Lilly and my other sister in and told them what my mum said and Lilly quickly defended her husband explaining to us that he is the sweetest person in the world. They got married; she left her job, closed down her boutique and moved to Lagos to her husband. I visited a few times and noticed something did not seem right" that she was gradually becoming a shadow of herself, she will say nothing to no one about the reason she had become so reserved. Then she lost her first baby and broke down totally, I moved in with her and tried to be there for her without understanding what was truly going on, my vibrant, beautiful, energetic, industrious sister was reduced to a shadow of herself and eventually passed on as a result of domestic violence. I remember sleeping over at Lilly's house and waking up to the angry voice of her husband at about 2am in the night, I listened to the conversation and realized that he had just returned from wherever at 2am and was screaming at the top of his voice and asking her why water spilled on the table in the living room. I was really upset and after he was done speaking with her, I asked to have a chat with him and I said to him "return her to us if you do not want to marry her anymore, before she became your wife she was someone's daughter, sister and aunty and we all care about her greatly.

    I tried to interrogate my sister thereafter but she won't give any details about what was going on, unknown to me he had a habit of beating her as often as he wanted as well as abusing her psychologically when they were alone. She eventually took ill and on her deathbed was able to open up on all that had happened amidst unconsciousness.

    While I was with her in the hospital, I found a lot of messages on her phone with the most painful ad scary conversations between them. He had beaten her and thrown her down the staircase and she had an injury in her head, he stole her phone as soon as she passed on because I had left at a point.

    The trauma that my family went through at the loss of my sister, the pain is inexplicable and six years later I still haven't recovered not to mention that my mother went into severe depression that later led to about two years of pseudo-dementia after the death of my sister. I was so down that I thought I will have a complete mental breakdown, the reality of the cause of her death made it even more painful, I was sure it was my fault, if I had been more around I would have noticed on time that she was being brutalized on a daily basis even with pregnancy, I would have understood why she hugged me like a savior the day I stood up to her husband on her behalf.

Is anyone still asking why I said I may never be a wife? It has been 7 years but I still feel the pain, I still remember her last words to me in the hospital before I travelled, she said "Victoria if I get well, take me to mummy's house, please don't take me back to that man's house" In her sleep, she kept saying things that were great revelations and sadly I left her for one day with my other sister and I got a call that she had passed away.

The months that followed, I will go to my office in the morning and keep a brave face while I return to my room and weep all night, beating myself and praying that I will wake up and realize it was a dream.

The death of Francis was yet another very painful experience for me, Francis was a child with special needs because he had cerebral palsy, he was brought to our orphanage home about 2 years and 5 months ago and even though we do not keep special children we accepted him. Francis had become part of the home and regarded as one of my children and suddenly he had running nose and died over night.

I was sure that was the end for me as I couldn't take it anymore, I felt it was my responsibility to save his life and I had failed as a mother. I told anyone that cared to listen that I was giving up the orphanage project. However when I returned to the home that evening and felt the love emanating from the other children I knew instantly that I was going nowhere.

Shame
Shame is just the devils way of accusing you and making you feel that `you have something that the world should not know; shame is a personal demon that limits you from living peacefully and growing beyond your mistakes.

The moment you realize that despite your mistakes, challenges and current situations, you are not the first to fall into that situation and you would not be the last to fall into that situation and there is nothing that has happened to you that has not happened to someone else before you.

Lilly was afraid and ashamed to let us know that her husband was violent, he blackmailed her into believing that if her marriage failed, she will be looked upon as a failure or as the cause. She was ashamed to mention the issues to us because she did not want us to say "we told you" He made her feel like something was wrong with her till she started believing that she is a lesser person.

Listen up, you are human so you are allowed to make mistakes, you are allowed to fail and you are allowed to be broke. The most important part of all of these is your ability to pick yourself up and try again. You are not in a competition with anyone and **most importantly you will not get help if you do not speak up and seek help.**

After my sister passed on, I realized the harm that we do to ourselves each time we measure ourselves and use other people's lives and opinions as our standards. I came to understand that for my sanity, I have to stop living to meet up with other people's lives or expectations and I should be able to accept that one mistake does not define my life.

We may and we would indeed go through challenges in life, but the big part is what we make out of these challenges; they are mostly a test that prepare us for greater things ahead and we must see challenges in that light rather than see challenges as deal breakers; of course I know advices like these are easier given than implemented.

Wining

In my introduction, I mentioned that pain could be

the greatest catalyst for growth and success if properly handled; I said this because I have been there on different levels and at the different times in my life.

For me the only way to overcome hurt is to prove to the people behind the hurt that I am a better person as I go. I worked twice as hard and became more determined than ever to achieve my dreams after I was told by my family that my future will be bleak simply because I studied Languages instead of Law I rose quickly above failure and regrets and eventually doors opened.

In the meantime, my siblings who initially withdrew all their support at the beginning and toughest times in my entrepreneurial dream had realized their wrong and they were trying to get in touch with me, I stayed away for very long but eventually found the grace to forgive and move on. Fast forward a few years later, I was popularly referred to as the one making the family proud. My dad and mum visited me once in Lagos at a time when my team was working on a diplomatic event for the Italian Navy and their embassy; the event took place on a ship called Carvour which birth in Nigeria.

I secured invitations for my parents and they attended the event being treated like first class citizens. When we got back home that evening, my father called me and blessed me. For the first time he had witnessed and had come to understand what my job entailed and he said "even though you do not have a lot of money, you have built relationships and a brand that will open doors for you and stand beyond money Victoria". I was ecstatic and emotional at the same time. I remembered my father's disposition initially and how hard I had worked to eventually get to the point where he was proud of me.

I got to a point where I could share my investment plans with my siblings and they would contribute financially to my projects, I even featured my sister in one of my TV productions, same sister whose husband thought I would end up a mediocre for studying Languages. She also anchored a spelling bee competition organized by my team and she could not stop speaking about how organized it was and the impact it made.

Tell me what else would be your definition of wining.

I am also determined to attain the apex of my career to make it impossible for my late sister's husband to keep out of my reach and make enough money to call him to order in the nearest future. I am slowly making peace with the fact that I will never see my sister again but I will also do everything within my reach to prevent other women from going through what she suffered and prevent families from losing their beloved daughters to beasts in that manner.

I would never be able to bring her back to life, but each time I save a woman or a man from falling victim to the same situation, I see that as my victory on her behalf. She said in her sleep while in the hospital "if only young girls will listen to their mothers, their lives will be a lot better" by this statement she was acknowledging the fact that she had made a mistake but she would feel better if other young women are saved from same circumstances.

Chapter 6:

Happiness, Self Love & Summary

I remember getting that call for a job interview at a multinational Oil Company in Nigeria, that I didn't apply to - for a job. I remember saying to myself how strange it felt and reminding myself that I wanted to stop mainstream work and begin to build the foundation for my charity which I had given myself a deadline to start at 25 years especially after the tragic loss of my sister.

I also remember the advice from my friend who doubles up as my business adviser, who encouraged me to give things a try. The job was nothing like where I was coming from, rolling in exotic cars and staying in five star hotels, I was now suddenly going to start resuming in an office in the morning to leave in the evening?

Then I reminded myself that I was done with the razmattazz and paparazzi because I wanted something deeper after the loss of my sister. Unknown to me, that interview will put me in contact with a mentor who eventually became my partner and pillar through the period of setting up the orphanage and the foundation. Today I run Qtaby Events alongside Life Fountain Orphanage Home and Jegede Paul Foundation. It feels as if I was born with the manual to do this effortlessly, I have a great team and we are making a difference, touching lives and defying odds.

I have however had to adhere to certain principles to keep the career going; hard work, resilience, consistency, and transparency. I have had to live within my means and I strive to always over impress my clients at every point. I have had to do jobs that were not financially profitable just to position my brand and make useful contacts, even though the world on the other side would envy the outcome without knowing the process I went through.

I will never be financially rewarded enough for the work that I put in but my reward comes when I help a youth out there find himself, define a career path and earn a decent living while making sense out of his life as an employee of my company. I feel fulfilled when I see the effect of my mentorship on another person's life.

Happiness for me lies in the eyes of my children at the orphanage the feeling is inexplicable when I am with them, the joy they feel, the excitement they show and the constant competition to get my attention. I am also at bliss when I am around loved ones and people who genuinely care about me be it family or friends, I am very sensitive and I can sense energies enough to recognize when gestures are sincere and when they are cosmetic. People need to discover what gives them Joy, it is relative and it differs from person to person but one useful advice I dish out is "never allow your happiness to depend on another person" discover or map out your own path to happiness. My mother taught me something growing up and it hasn't left me till date. She said to me " my daughter, anyone that has the ability to make you angry is stronger than you and has power over you so the person can decide to upset you at will and chooses when you are happy and when you are unhappy" Give no one such powers over your emotions. I have since trained myself to only feign anger but never get angry so people around me get to wonder about my capacity and ability to quickly change from a fire spark to a giggling darling.

MY INFLUENCES

I believe a lot in mentorship and in mentoring people, I know that I can never mirror my life in another person's life, I understand absolutely that I am full of flaws as well as I stumble along life so I try to pass across what I consider positive to my mentees just the same way I try to only pick up positivity from my mentors.

My life influences came from my mother and my sister at the early stage and as I grew older, I also met a few more people that inspired me a lot for different reasons. I believe we all have to learn from those who have already gone through the roads that we are now walking.

Speaking about being mentored by my mother, I have never seen a woman so loving and humble, so soft spoken and yet so firm, so conservative but very generous; a woman goal getter that knows what she wants and will stop at nothing to get them, my mother will always have a short, mid-term and long-term goal and an execution plan yet she is flexible enough to know when it isn't working and a change of plan is needed. A career woman that knew that her first job is her home, husband and children, I grew up realising that it will be an uphill task to mirror all these attributes but I will like to imbibe a few of them.

I have been influenced a lot by my partner in the foundation, Mr. Jegede Paul who has consistently proven that it is important to stand true to your commitments in partnerships despite complicated challenges. I have learnt a lot from Ofer Lapid the CEO of Gear House South Africa who despite owning the largest events logistics company in the world, has maintained a very 'SIMPLE" personality and manages to balance that with crude business ethics and by the way I ask him for one sentence to hold on to each time we meet. In all, no man is an island and no man will know it all, except you decide to make all of life's mistakes in the course of your sojourn, you will need to discover that one person or people whose visions align with yours and they have successfully gone through the path that you are currently taking.

Resolution and PHILOSOPHY

I wish that I learnt on time that it is okay to be selfish. Selfish in terms of ensuring that you are okay, safe, well and stable enough to help others be okay after all a drowning man cannot help another to shore. I am strong and different but I will be exhausted if I use all my strength in holding others up without ensuring that I am also up. I have resolved to live before killing myself to ensure that other people live, I have resolved to touch the world beginning from myself and touch lives beginning from my life... didn't they say that charity begins at home? My philosophy has always been: Live and lets live, you can't judge me when you haven't worn my shoes and vice versa, *give everyone a second chance then uproot permanently if they screw it again*. I have realized that I cannot do much on my own and so I make use of the people around me as they have become my greatest assets, above all I ensure that I handover to God whatever seems beyond me and he has always figured it out effortlessly. Never underestimate anyone in life as you are not totally in control of the road that life will take you. Relationships are your first capital, nurture them like you will nurture your business.

Remember: Your life is a book that only you can write, make it a BESTSELLER.

Outro

I am fortunate to be an entrepreneur at a time when I can sit in a village in Africa and reach out to clients all over the world in ten minutes through an email, when I can create adverts and tailor them towards specific target demography from the comfort of my home. For my business social media is a great working tool and I am fortunate to have been born in this era.

I am also aware of the pressures that exist as a result of this social media era but I have chosen to determine my own pace. I see a lot of people living perfect lives online and I see a lot of people wishing that life was theirs. Put in the work that you need to, believe in the process and wait on your time. People on social media are showing you the life that they want you to see, they are not showing you their life as it is. Rather than spend time wishing you were in another person's shoes, you could rather spend time building your empire with the use of social media.

The force behind the vision and the vision itself are beyond me, so even if I wanted to stop, these two are going to keep me going against all odds. I have realized that my attitude will take me where my talent will not and so I make an extra effort to carry the right attitude around along with me as the most important fashion element that I put on daily. *I have got two choices in life, to be successful or to be successful*; ever since I realized this fact, I realized the extent of the responsibility that I have especially because I MEASURE MY SUCCESS BY THE NUMBER OF LIVES THAT I AM ABLE TO IMPACT ON THIS JOURNEY CALLED MY LIFE.

SHINE

Listen to me, woman or man, boy or girl, white or black; wherever you find yourself, let your light shine! Do not shine your light for your use alone but let your light shine so bright that everyone can benefit from its' brightness. Do not let anyone dim your light as you have the sole responsibility to keep your light shining, to reach your potentials and to prove your worth to yourself primarily and to everyone else.

You are strong, you are powerful, there is greatness in you, you are an achiever; let no one stop you. No one and nothing can stop you besides yourself. The world is your stage, go on and play your role.

There is nothing wrong with being different, being different is a niche, being different is the new cool as long as you are being different positively.

Stand out, it is okay to be misunderstood, it is okay not to follow the norm, you can actually create a norm with your own signature style.

I have spent the last 30 years of my life being different, and I have had people seeking to understand how and why I choose to be different and I sometimes marvel at how I survive in my difference; then I remember that every great invention started from someone who did something different and investigated his difference till he made sense out of it.

With your eyes on the goal, you will achieve and attain that apex that you so desire. Ride on STRONG, Woman or Man, your determination maybe mistaken for madness sometimes, that is not such a bad idea after all, because you can then write a book and name it "The Diary of a Mad Black (or white), Woman (or Man).

My Favourite Quotes

"Seeming successful is sweet, being successful is sweeter but hardwork is the key that opens these doors"
- ***Victoria Nkong***

"Do not let your self-worth to be determined by people's perception of you. You were made for greatness. There is a star in you."
- ***Victoria Nkong***

"Keep your circles closed, some people come around just to know what makes you thick. Keep them clueless till you are sure of their motive."
- ***Victoria Nkong***

"It is okay to help emerging brands to grow, they are not your competition, they are your support system."
- ***Victoria Nkong***

"Sometimes you need to look back at your achievements and celebrate yourself, then remind yourself of how you achieved them and strategize for new wins."
- *Victoria Nkong*

"Everyone has a" story" from their past but what makes your STORY worth it is what you have made of your STORY despite your "story".
- *Victoria Nkong*

"My attitude births my dreams, I sleep long enough to dream and I wake early enough to achieve my dreams. FOCUS."
- *Victoria Nkong*

"I do not have all I want but I have all I need: A sound mind, passion and determination."
- *Victoria Nkong*

About The Author

Victoria Nkong (C.E.O Qtaby Events) is a multilingual Entertainment consultant, An Events & Content Producer, Talent Manager, Public Speaker, PR strategist with a strong interest in supporting less privilege children and youth, she has been involved in events production and entertainment for over ten years and has been running charity projects for about five years now. Her break into entertainment was through the prestigious **KORA** All Africa Music Awards as bilingual presenter.

As a talent Manager and PR strategist, Victoria has worked with most of the big artists and personalities around Africa and the world over.

Besides KORA, she has also successfully produced a number of world-class events like the Opening Ceremony of the International African Athletic Competition, Headies Awards, Bidvest Chairmanship Awards SA, AFRIMA and several others.

As a Philantropist, she is on the board of trustee of Jegede Paul Foundation, she is the Administrator and mother to the children at Life Fountain Orphanage Home. She is also the brain behind the annual "Slum Invasion" outreach to slums and Share your closet for widows.

After co-authoring a best-selling anthology with 20 other women from different continents.

Made in the USA
Coppell, TX
03 April 2023